Guarding and Protecting your Prophetic Word

How to Activate and Enforce your Prophetic Word

Discerning between a True and a False Prophecy

Mammah u are blessed

By Daniel Amoateng.

Forwarded by Bishop E. O. ANSAH.

Guarding and Protecting your Prophetic Word.
How to Activate and Enforce your Prophetic Word
Discerning between a True and a False Prophecy

By Daniel Amoateng.

www.ingenepublications.co.uk

© 2011, Ingene Publications

A division of the Ingene Group

ISBN : 978-0-9562534-2-2

Printed in the United Kingdom
Marketed & Distributed by
Ingene Publications
63 FERNHEAD ROAD,
MAIDA VALE, W9
LONDON.

You can do an online purchase of more copies of this book and
future material by the same author from
www.amazon.com or www.ingenepublications.co.uk

Table of Contents

Dedication: This book is dedicated to all who seek the true knowledge of GOD and understanding of the Great Commission. Also to my entire ministry partners who have supported me all these years.

Acknowledgements

I thank the Almighty GOD our Heavenly Father for his grace and love towards me and giving me insight to bless his people with this work. I thank my Parents Dr & Mrs Amoateng and other members of the family. Monica Lutta, thank you for all your efforts. Thank you to my fellow co-labourers in the vineyard of GOD, Bishop Ansah and Wife, Pastor Tony and wife, Prophet Ernest Owusu and all the pastors of Kingdom life ministries as well as the members not forgetting the all night community. To friends and mentors. To all the team at Ingene Publications and my Publisher Thank you so much. I will also use this opportunity to thank Pastor Tunji Ogunjimi for linking me with the right people to handle this book. And to all those who have impacted me in one way or the other who I have not mentioned your names but my heart says thank you to all of you.

Forward

The Mark of a true Prophet is that his words come to pass. That is the key reason I undertook the task of writing the Forward for this illuminating book. In our day, where one has to be careful with who a true Prophet is, Prophet Daniel Amoateng has distinguished himself as one who does not only "talk the talk" but also "walk the walk".

I have humbly sat under his Spirit-filled Prophetic ministry with signs to back it up. Even as his Spiritual Father for many years I have come to a conclusion that his gifting are God given and the signs "could only be God!"

In his book "Guarding and Protecting your Prophetic Word", Prophet Daniel, with his impeccable divine insight and wisdom (Literally four times his age) he has:

- Unravelled the mystery surrounding delayed fulfilment of Prophecies and also how to accelerate or activate your Prophetic word.
- Highlighted How to identify your Prophetic gift and effectively sharpen it to affect your generation.
- Shared some of the unbelievable oracles the Holy Spirit spoke through him concerning individuals and nations.

I deem this book a Prophetic Manual indeed!!! It is a must – read

Bishop E. O. Ansah
General Overseer
Kingdom Life Ministries (KLM)

Book Endorsements

I believe it is about time that some understanding was brought to this subject. I am glad Prophet Daniel Amoateng is throwing light on this. I believe in his calling and know him as a man of integrity. Bishop O.A. Bernard **(Presiding Bishop Praise Valley & Associate Churches, Holland).**

This book will show you how to discover and follow GOD's plan for your life. A must read for every believer desiring to see the demonstration of GOD's power in these last days. I believe in the Prophetic gifting in Prophet Daniel. **(Mr Edward M. Turay. High Commissioner of Sierra Leone to the United Kingdom and Northern Ireland).**

Prophet Daniel is an unmitigated Prophet of GOD through whom I have learnt that indeed we still have amongst us Prophets of GOD who can work exploits like the Prophet of old. His zeal and dedication in serving the most high GOD is incomprehensible. I have been truly blessed by his ministry. **Richard Olufisan Magnus (Solicitor of the Supreme Court of England and Wales. Managing Partner Still Waters Global Consulting).**

The demonstration and use of the Prophetic is at the core of the Holy Book and it is an important guide. In today's church, this important tenet has been corrupted and various counterfeits abound. I look to Prophet Daniel Amoateng to dissect this important guide to our faith and other invaluable guidance on the subject matter. **Tosin Adewuyi, Managing Director and Senior Country Officer Nigeria JP Morgan.**

This is a timely manual needed to set the Prophetic records straight in our generation. **(Daniel Amoateng's Dad) Dr Gabriel Amoateng-Boahen, Chaplain, University of Chicago Hospital, USA.**

A comprehensive guide to help you understand the hidden truths about Prophecy. A must read for every believer desiring the manifestation of the Glory of GOD. **Abi Sanni Trinity Solicitors, London UK.**

If you don't know where you are going in life no matter how fast you run, you might not make it to any destination. Remember! The manifestation of "Thus Sayest the Lord" is a necessity which therefore makes this book a requirement towards fulfilling your GOD given assignment on Earth. **Prophet Ernest Owusu Kingdom Life Ministries. London, UK.**

Fulfilling the Prophetic message is conditional **(Daniel Amoateng's Mum) Mrs Agatha Amoeteng-Boahem C.E.O Maranatha Health Services, Ghana.**

Such an incredible insight. A must get for every believer or unbeliever. Prophet Brian Jones **(Founder Brian Jones Outreach Inc. London, UK.)**

This is a fascinating masterpiece. Carefully rendered to address a difficult and important subject to the Body of Christ. It is a great eye-opener for the Body of Christ. **Joe and Renee Aryeetey. (Directors Reino Group).**

Believe it or not we at the Ingene Publications do not take on a job if we do not believe in the work. This one here by Prophet Daniel was an exceptional work, a God-sent piece, it blew us away. everyone on the team took a liking to the book at first glance. Personally, I believe this book will change the life of whoever reads, understands and does what it says. It has changed mine and I highly recommend. Olu-davids Boboye **(Chief Editor Ingene Publications).**

Preface

This piece of heavenly writing carries the information that you need to acquire a full understanding of the Prophetic Ministry and the fulfilment of a prophecy. As I travel the road in the Prophetic Ministry, I have discovered that many people including believers and unbelievers have battled with the question: why does a prophecy take a long time to be fulfilled or does not come to pass at all even though it was delivered accurately from a reliable prophet? It is based on this precept that through the inspiration and the guidance of the Holy Spirit, God laid it passionately on my heart and spiritually downloaded the answers we need in the Body of Christ. I will carefully show you the necessary processes needed to make the transition from 'It shall come to pass' to 'and it came to pass', because these two statements are entirely different and both occur in the Bible.

Across the globe, from Africa to Asia, America to Australia, Cairo to Cape Town, London to Las Vegas, Zambia to Zimbabwe you will see the definite need for a prophetic word in a person's life and how it must be fulfilled. This prophetic manual seeks to show you what to do when you receive a prophetic word and how to fulfil your prophetic word. The difference between prophecies and Words of Knowledge is the way prophetic instructions rely on prophetic signs and tokens to judge true and false prophecy.

Whether you live in a palace, prison, plantation or pit you need a sure prophetic word from God to shift your life to the next level and that is what I call "thus saith the LORD". With Scriptural support, I will explain the significance of prophetic protection so you can recognise in your own life those situations and crises that need both fasting and prayer. You know from the Scripture that Jesus Christ said to his disciples:

> *"However, this kind does not go out except by prayer and fasting"*
>
> Matthew 17:21

The LORD means that not every issue must be addressed with fasting; however, there are some issues that obviously and absolutely need prayer and fasting. I will carefully show the kinds of circumstances and issues in your life that call for fasting. These answers the following questions: what is fasting? when should you fast? how to fast wisely? the different types of fasting and what is the significance of fasting? The main influence of prayer on prophecy is also carefully studied. This prophetic manual will also outline, carefully and accurately, the prophecies concerning the next decade and what we should expect to see. This is also coupled with many incredible and awesome testimonies associated with my years of operating in the Prophetic Office that will catapult your faith to the next level and renew your confidence in the Prophetic Ministry. Once you infuse your intelligence with this heavenly knowledge, your life will never be the same.

Chapter 1

Introduction to the Prophetic Ministry/Prophetic Office

I will start by explaining prophecy. According to the Oxford Advanced Learners dictionary, *prophecy* is defined as "knowledge of the future obtained from a divine source". The Hebrew word for prophecy is *nabuwah* which means to speak by inspiration. The Greek word for prophecy is *propheteia*, which means to speak about the future. Therefore, according to the dictionary, a prophet is defined as someone who speaks by divine inspiration about the future. The Hebrew word for a prophet is *nabiy* which means an inspired man. The Greek is *prophetes* which is an inspired speaker. In the Greek, the word *pro* means before or fore and that is why we have the words such as profile or prologue. So, a prophet can be seen as someone who speaks before something happens. Now, a prophet speaks under the inspiration of God to make known the ways, agendas, ideas and intentions of God to humanity. God is so faithful that he reveals to us not only his purposes but also the hidden secrets that we ought to know. He reveals himself through his servants, the Prophets.

> *"And he gave some, apostles; and some, prophets; and some, evangelists; and some, pastors and teachers; for the perfecting of the saints, for the work of the ministry, for the edifying of the body of Christ"*
>
> Ephesians 4:11-12

In the book of *Ephesians,* Apostle Paul introduced the Fivefold Ministry which he said helps to perfect and edify the Body of Christ of which the Prophetic Ministry is part. The reason why the prophetic ministry is delicate as well as sensitive is because it exposes the devices of the Enemy and over the years the Enemy has tried to scandalise and attack it in many ways. In these latter days, the New Testament Church, as stated by the Apostle Paul, is built on the foundations of the Apostles and Prophets.

> *"And are built upon the foundation of the apostles and prophets, Jesus Christ himself being the chief corner stone"*
>
> Ephesians 2:20

We are in the last days and the prophetic ministry plays an important role in the life of the believer.

Chapter 1

*"And it shall come to pass afterward, that I will pour
out my spirit upon all flesh; and your sons and your
daughters shall prophesy, your old men shall dream
dreams, your young men shall see visions"*

Joel 2:28

This is an inspired prophecy by Prophet Joel. The 'sons and
daughters will prophesy' means prophecy in these latter days
is essential and hence vital to the Body of Christ. The Bible
now confirms that the LORD will not do anything until he
reveals to his servants the Prophets.

*"Surely the Lord GOD will do nothing, but he
revealeth his secret unto his servants the prophets"*

Amos 3:7

The prophetic office or someone who operates in the
prophetic office is one who by divine appointment is
ordained to reveal the secrets of God. This gives us the means
to judge between a true and false Prophet/prophecy.
Prophecy should always be directed towards the revealing of
the agenda of God. Since prophecy is dedicated to helping
people focus on the will of God, it helps prepare us for the
work of ministry and thereby brings perfection to every area
of our lives. Any aim other than these, makes the authen-
ticity of a Prophet/prophecy doubtful. Furthermore, there is

a clear distinction between someone who operates in the prophetic office and one who operates with the gift of prophecy. Every believer can be endowed with the gift of prophecy to speak and declare about the future under inspiration but a Prophet is one who completely, absolutely and totally is ordained specifically to prophesy and operate in the prophetic office. This is confirmed in 1Cor 12 which refers to the gifts of the spirit of which the gift of prophecy is a part.

> *"To another the working of miracles; to another prophecy; to another discerning of spirits; to another divers kinds of tongues; to another the interpretation of tongues"*
>
> 1 Corinthians 12:10

The Scripture emphasizes that we should covet prophecy, so every believer's desire to prophesy is important but not all are Prophets. When you can prophesy, it doesn't make you a Prophet. Not until you are fully ordained in the prophetic office do you become a Prophet, living in a car does not make you a car.

> *"Wherefore, brethren, covet to prophesy, and forbid not to speak with tongues"*
>
> 1 Corinthians 14:39

So long as you are a believer, you must have an ultimate desire to prophesy.

Word Of Knowledge

The other aspect of the prophetic ministry is the Word of Knowledge. A Word of Knowledge is a spiritual gift given by the Holy Spirit; it is factual in nature and brings immediate realization and understanding. All Words of Knowledge are prophetic in the sense of being instructive, insightful and/or inspiring. A Word of Knowledge is the ability to call out a person that you have never seen before accurately by name (first or maiden name), know a person's telephone number, date of birth, birthplace, and place of residence, school attended, father's name, mother's name, relatives' names, account number, etc. A prophetic Word of Knowledge is tailored by the Holy Spirit and gives a clear conviction to the person receiving it such that the person knows that God will confirm His word. It demonstrates that God knows everything about us and thus He knew us before we were formed in the wombs of our mothers and even He has numbered the hairs on our head. Many people have come to see Word of Knowledge as prophecy but it is only designed to bring more clarity to the prophecy.

"For to one is given by the Spirit the word of wisdom;
to another the word of knowledge by the same Spirit"
1 Corinthians 12:8

In my years of operating in the prophetic office, God has used me tremendously to work deeply with Words of Knowledge. This has helped people learn that God knows everything about them. Prophecy given in connection with a Word of Knowledge solidifies that Word. At a prophetic conference in London, United Kingdom, I remember ministering to a woman. I told her that she was being healed by God of a severe heart condition and I saw God's angels operating on her heart and God giving her a new heart. As I came close to her and told her what I saw she was amazed. She confirmed that she had received surgical operations twice but her condition did not improve. The doctors had told her that she only had a few months to live. As I continued to minister to her, God used me to call out two names of people connected to her who were also being healed. She confirmed that the two names I called out were her sisters' names and that they both lived in Africa. She told me they were both ill and one of them had her hand amputated due to diabetes. This really made her believe in the healing that God was bringing her way. I later pointed out to her the secret behind their suffering. The Enemy had tried to bring premature death their way because of a crisis in her paternal family. God used me to call out their father's name and where he used to live. I described the colour of a building he had built.

Almost a year later, I went back to the same church and I

met the same lady I ministered to in the Word of Knowledge. She is now healed and strong by the glory of God.

A Word of Knowledge causes shock and panic and erases doubt and unbelief even in those most sceptical about prophecy. It helps introduce people to the Kingdom of God. In John 4, Jesus Christ at the well in Samaria used the Word of Knowledge to convert the woman and convince her that he was the Messiah.

> *"Jesus saith unto her, Go, call thy husband, and come hither. The woman answered and said, I have no husband. Jesus said unto her, Thou hast well said, I have no husband: For thou hast had five husbands; and he whom thou now hast is not thy husband: in that saidst thou truly. The woman saith unto him, Sir, I perceive that thou art a prophet"*
>
> John 4:16-19

This Word of Knowledge left the woman in shock and she ran about to tell everyone that she had seen a prophet and he was the Messiah. One word of knowledge can help draw thousands to God.

In John 1, there is a dialogue between Jesus Christ, Philip and Nathaniel. Here, Nathaniel is convinced that Jesus is indeed the son of God and the promised King of Israel.

"The day following Jesus would go forth into Galilee, and findeth Philip, and saith unto him, Follow me. Now Philip was of Bethsaida, the city of Andrew and Peter. Philip findeth Nathaniel, and saith unto him, We have found him, of whom Moses in the law, and the prophets, did write, Jesus of Nazareth, the son of Joseph. And Nathaniel said unto him, Can there any good thing come out of Nazareth? Philip saith unto him, Come and see. Jesus saw Nathaniel coming to him, and saith of him, Behold an Israelite indeed, in whom is no guile! Nathaniel saith unto him, Whence knowest thou me? Jesus answered and said unto him, Before that Philip called thee, when thou wast under the fig tree, I saw thee. Nathaniel answered and saith unto him, Rabbi, thou art the Son of God; thou art the King of Israel"

John 1:43-49

In John 1:47, when Philip told Nathaniel that he had found the Messiah, Nathaniel doubted if anything good could ever come out of Nazareth. Jesus' first statement to Nathaniel was "Behold an Israelite indeed in whom is no guile." Nathaniel then asked Jesus "when knowest thou me?" Jesus correctly stated the home town of Nathaniel and that he was a true Jewish man. That is why Nathaniel asked Jesus, 'where he knew him from?' So when a Prophet calls you out by your address, place of residence or birthplace it is nothing new, Jesus did likewise. Also, Jesus continued the conversation by telling Nathaniel that he saw Nathaniel under the fig which means Words of Knowledge help point out many things from the past. This later helped Nathaniel to believe the prophecy that Moses, in the Law, and the Prophets wrote about Jesus of Nazareth.

I remember in 2007 I was in Germany, to be precise in Hamburg, ministering. I called out to a woman and told her, 'God was giving her a baby girl' because I saw by revelation that she was barren and she needed the fruit of the womb. She was happy to receive what belonged to her because she had been married for eight years and had never given birth. I saw by revelation that the Enemy had marked a boundary and on it was written three months, which I interpreted to her that the Enemy doesn't want her to carry her conception beyond the third month. She confirmed that any time she conceived, at the third month she would dream in the middle of the night of a man trying to make love to her. When she had that dream early in the morning she would find drops of blood and she would realise the pregnancy has been aborted. I told her that GOD had stopped that spirit who was responsible for miscarriage with His Mighty hand and that after a year she would have a daughter to carry. By the grace of God exactly a year later she had a baby girl, to the glory of God. What really made that woman have a cheerful attitude at the time she received the prophetic word was that the spirit behind her calamity was identified and that what she had experienced over the years was revealed. She was assured that God knew exactly what she was going through.

Some time ago, a friend asked me, "Prophet why is it that modern day Prophets prophesy to people by calling out names but in the Bible days the Prophets in the Old Testament only prophesied about the future without calling out a person's name?" When I heard the question I had a good laugh and told him he needs to read and understand his Bible. I pointed out to him that long before the Israelites were taken into captivity by the Babylonians, Prophet Isaiah revealed that after a period of seventy years in exile God would use a king by the name of Cyrus to bring his people out of captivity. This was about one hundred and fifty years before the Israelites were out of captivity and it came to pass that God used King Cyrus to free His people.

> *"That saith of Cyrus, He is my shepherd, and shall perform all my pleasure: even saying to Jerusalem, Thou shalt be built; and to the temple, Thy foundation shall be laid"*
>
> Isaiah 44:28

Word of Knowledge and prophecy go hand in hand. I pray

that God gives you strength and the power to cause all the prophetic words you have received to come to pass in Jesus' name. In the next decade, which starts from 2010, there are going to be dangerous natural disasters that will claim many lives. Some of these disasters include earthquakes, floods, landslides, volcanic eruptions, famine, tornadoes and hurricanes. The year 2010 will also mark the beginning of the recovery of the world's economy but the great part of it will be shifted to Asia. This shift will cause many people from Asia and the Middle East to take over major organizations and business across Europe, America and Africa.

The light and horn of the continent of Africa will be exalted and many nations in Africa will become a force to reckon with. Great men and organisations will emerge from Africa, and God will cause some Africans to head many worldwide organisations. There will also be a noticeable increase in plane crashes, trains and car crashes. I pray that you will not become a victim. Some of these crashes will claim the lives of great persons. Different government policies will spark unnecessary tensions across nations because these policies will not be favourable to most people. There will be shocking news across news channels, stories that will cause panic. I urge all believers across the nations to come together to intercede for the youth, because youth crimes will escalate but by the power of prayer these crimes will be defeated.

The good part of this whole thing about the youth is that God will cause a great shift for the youth to take over in every area of the world's organisations from ministry, entertainment, sports, politics, business etc. There will be a loss of great names, leaders, major stars and celebrities from entertainment to fashion to sports, in religious and political organisations. Divorces and separations in marriage will rise and even Christian marriages will be under threat, including those of great preachers, who will be scandalised, but God will sustain His people.

This is a great call for all of us to pray. The best thing that will happen is the increase in Christian missionaries across the continents and to places that have never heard the gospel before. Places where it was difficult to preach the Gospel before will have their doors and gates opened but the persecution will continue. This will be seen in the growth of faith based television stations and networks. Their broadcast will cover vast areas and across many remote regions of the world.

There will be a major wealth transfer to the Body of Christ, and also to places and people who were least likely. I want to admonish all intercessors to help pray for the Middle East, to stop all attacks, bombings and wars that spread across nations and cause other nations to become victims of suicide attacks.

Chapter 2

Guarding and protecting your Prophetic word The Significance and Dynamics of Prayer

I have ministered in so many places and I've also met a lot of people both believers and non-believers. Both have one question in common: Why their prophecies have not come to pass? Most people have received several prophecies but without the expected results. Sometimes they agree that the prophecy was accurate but they wonder why there has been no manifestation. There are many times when a prophet will prophesy and the individual will confirm that they have received the same prophecy from other prophets but still no manifestation of the prophecy. The question is, why did the prophecy not come to pass? The answer to that question is my purpose for writing this book. Beloved, there is a clear difference between "It shall come to pass" and "It has come to pass".

There is a process that occurs between the period when a prophecy is spoken, "it shall come to pass", and its manifestation, "it has come to pass". When you read your Bible, you will often find the two statements above. The problem many people have with the prophetic ministry and why most people are angry with the prophetic ministry is a lack of understanding of the transition between these two statements. Many prophets fail to show or carefully direct the individual who has received the prophecy how to bring about this transition. Failure to recognise what happens between these two statements will always lead you to doubt prophecies. In this chapter, I will thoroughly explain the necessary processes responsible for graduating from "It shall come to pass" to "It has come to pass". What needs to be done when a prophetic word is released, is for the receiver of the word to go into battle, wage war and fight using the prophetic word. I will show you scenarios from the Bible as well as practical examples. Beloved, when you receive a prophetic word, that's not the end of it, you will surely recognise that when you haven't received any word you are free. The Enemy doesn't know what God is about to do in your life or what is about to materialize. When the prophetic utterance or word is released, it is an announcement of the purpose of God concerning your life and shows you what He is ready to do. When this announcement is made, not only do good people or God's people or angels hear it but the

Devil also hears it. The Devil seeks to steal, kill and destroy. He strives in many ways to sabotage and stop the manifestation of the word. So, when you receive a prophetic word, guard your lips and be careful not to broadcast it. Beloved, can't you think back to when you were doing very well until you received a prophetic word, and then all hell broke loose in your life? This is because the Enemy is angry about what you have received.

"Surely the Lord GOD will do nothing, but he revealeth his secret unto his servants the prophets"
Amos 3:7

Amos makes it clear that GOD only reveals to his servants the Prophets what He is ready to do. The prophetic word being spoken in your life, even though it is accurate, unless you go to war and battle with the word in prayer, the time when it can manifest may pass. The first thing to do when you receive a prophetic word is to enter into serious prayers, instead of telling everyone your word. Even if it is about you receiving a promotion, travelling, being healed or becoming prosperous, you ought to pray because it is prayer that will superimpose the agenda and idea of heaven on the affairs of humanity. You pray to guard and protect the prophetic word and at the same time ensure it will happen within its stipulated time. After Elijah prophesied to Ahab a coming abundance of rain, he then began the process of bringing the word released into manifestation: he went to Mount Carmel to pray.

> *"And Elijah said unto Ahab, Get thee up, eat and drink; for there is a sound of abundance of rain. So Ahab went up to eat and to drink. And Elijah went up to the top of Carmel; and he cast himself down upon the earth, and put his face between his knees"*
>
> 1Kings 18:41-42

Elijah was considered an authentic prophet; however, when he told Ahab that there was a sound of the abundance of the rain it did not rain immediately. This is the same thing that happens to us when God gives us a prophetic word through His prophets about a coming breakthrough but there seems to be no sign of the manifestation of the promise. It is when there is no sign of the promise that you enter into the place of prayer because God will make a way where there seems to be no way. Imagine Elijah praying and the servant moving up and down seven times to check for a sign of rain. He could have been frustrated but he held on to the word because faithful is He who has promised and surely He will do it.

> *And said to his servant, Go up now, look toward the sea. And he went up, and looked, and said, There is nothing. And he said, Go again seven times. And it*

came to pass at the seventh time, that he said, Behold, there ariseth a little cloud out of the sea, like a man's hand. And he said, Go up, say unto Ahab, Prepare thy chariot, and get thee down, that the rain stop thee not. And it came to pass in the mean while, that the heaven was black with clouds and wind, and there was a great rain. And Ahab rode, and went to Jezreel. And the hand of the LORD was on Elijah; and he girded up his loins, and ran before Ahab to the entrance of Jezreel.

1 Kings 18:43-46

In the same manner, when you receive a prophecy you have a part to play in the manifestation of that prophecy. You have the power of prayer and just like Elijah you can call those things which are not as though they were (Romans 4:17). In Psalm 119:89, we are told that God's word is settled in heaven. It is however with much business and painful effort that we can bring that word to come to pass.

For a dream cometh through the multitude of business; and a fool's voice is known by multitude of words.

Ecclesiastes 5:3

If there is something that you need to do to put your life in order, then you must start dealing with it while it is still a small fire. Don't wait until it is a blaze to start putting it out. You may need to get things cleaned up, be it in your marriage or your finances. Your dreams and visions will come to pass but with much business and effort. It is much easier to take small but consistent steps to put things in order than it is to stay in bondage. Part of having your dreams and visions come to pass, is that you also must remain expectant. Expectation is synonymous with anticipation, looking forward to, looking out for or hoping for something. It also means waiting or preparing for a promise.

"I had fainted, unless I had believed to see the
goodness of the LORD in the land of the living."
Psalm 27:13

Waiting in expectation for a promise involves active spirituality, you need to stay aggressive. By aggressive, I mean aggressive Godly action through spoken words, prayer and walking in righteousness. The Kingdom of God suffers violence but the violent take it by force. You must stay focused and believe that the promises of God are true and they shall come to pass but it takes action on your part.

"Elias was a man subject to like passions as we are,
and he prayed earnestly that it might not rain: and

it rained not on the earth by the space of three years and six months. And he prayed again, and the heaven gave rain, and the earth brought forth her fruit."

James 5:17-18

The Scripture above shows prayer as the main foundation for the manifestation of the prophetic word released by Elijah. He prayed that it would not rain and he prayed *earnestly* that there would be an abundance of rain and it was so. The word earnest means perseverance, continuance and persistence. In other words, pray tirelessly until the purpose for the prayer has been seen through. It was after the seventh time that Elijah's servant told him that he saw a cloud the size of a man's hand. God will always confirm His word by a man or through a man.

You can also see that Elijah and Ahab did different things when the word for the abundance of rain was released. Ahab went to eat and drink while Elijah went to pray. This is quite similar to two groups of people in the Church today. There are those who eat and party as they are happy with their prophetic word, and there are others who will pray until their prophetic word comes to pass.

1 Kings Chapter 18 speaks about prophecy from the very first verse. God gave a Word to Elijah about the promise of rain, and then there was the battle on Mount Carmel

between Prophet Elijah and the prophets of Baal. And, it was not until that battle at Mount Carmel had ended that Elijah's prophecy came to pass, in 1 Kings 18:45.

I remember in the year 2008, a lady called Georgina called me from Australia and asked me to pray for her because she had stomach complications. She told me that she had been to the hospital and it was determined that she had bacteria in her stomach. She had been prescribed medication but whenever she went for follow up check-ups, the number of bacteria increased. She was so worried because the medication was supposed to make her better. Instead, the bacteria were multiplying and she was getting worse. She told her brother, who lived in London, about it. It happened that he had been attending some of the prophetic meetings that I was holding and he suggested that she call me. When Georgina called me and told me about the complication, God spoke to me that it was an abdominal cancer plot designed against her. God revealed to me that she had travelled two months earlier to her hometown and that was where the attack began. She confirmed her travel and also that the doctors had told her when she went to the hospital that if the condition in her stomach wasn't dealt with, it could lead to cancer. God, through prophetic revelation to me, gave her a word of assurance that she was going to be healed.

When the word came, Georgina and I embarked on a fourteen day fast from 6am–6pm daily. I asked her to follow specific prophetic directions after she had eaten. Beloved, we were strong and consistent in prayer. After the fourteen days of prayer and fasting, she went for a check-up. To her surprise, it took a very long time for her results to come back. It would normally have taken a week to get her results back but, this time around, it took almost a month. She was disturbed by the time it was taking for her results to come back, so she kept calling me. But I believed that an awesome miracle had taken place. On the day she was asked to go in for her results, they proved negative and there were no bacteria in her stomach. The main reason for this awesome testimony is to illustrate the significance of prayer and fasting as well as the consistency of prayer upon receiving a prophetic word.

Furthermore, the significance of prayer is seen in the life of Daniel. Daniel understood the importance of prayer through the study of the Words of Prophecy spoken by Prophet Jeremiah concerning the captivity of Israel which was to last seventy years. He lived in that era, but he found out that although seventy years had elapsed the Israelites were still in exile. In order for him to ensure the prophetic word, he had to enter into prayer and fasting

"In the first year of his reign I Daniel understood by books the number of the years, whereof the word of

the LORD came to Jeremiah the prophet that he would accomplish seventy years in the desolations of Jerusalem. And I set my face unto the Lord God, to seek by prayer and supplications, with fasting, and sackcloth, and ashes"

Daniel 9:2-3

Dear reader, I want you to answer a few questions here. Since the seventy years had elapsed and the Israelites were still in exile, could it be that Prophet Jeremiah was a false prophet? Did he give a false prophecy? The answer to both questions is an emphatic "no". Why, then, didn't the prophecy come to pass automatically? This means prophecy is not fulfilled just by utterance but someone has to engage in spiritual warfare. Daniel fasted for 21 days and prayed, and yet the archangel Michael had to engage in warfare with the prince of Persia. This shows the prince of Persia was the one responsible for hindering the prophecy from coming to pass. Daniel's prayers were sabotaged because the prince of Persia, a spirit being, worked so hard to stop the Word from being fulfilled.

Yea, whiles I was speaking in prayer, even the man Gabriel, whom I had seen in the vision at the beginning, being caused to fly swiftly, touched me about the time of the evening oblation. And he informed me, and talked with me, and said, O Daniel, I am now come forth to give thee skill and understanding. At the beginning of thy supplications the commandment came forth, and I am come to shew thee; for thou art greatly beloved: therefore understand the matter, and consider the vision.

Daniel 9:21-23

Chapter 3

The Significance of Fasting

Fasting is defined as voluntarily abstaining from food for spiritual purposes. Prayer and fasting often go hand in hand, but this is not always the case. You can pray without fasting. It is, however, when prayer and fasting are combined and dedicated to God's glory that they reach their full effectiveness. Having a dedicated time of prayer and fasting is not a way of manipulating God into doing what you desire. Rather, it is simply positioning you to focus and rely on God for the strength, provision, wisdom and power you need.

Different Types of Fasting

There are different types of fasting and I normally recommend to people that they should fast according to their strength. Fasting is not just an act of starving yourself. Rather, in order to achieve the purpose for which you are fasting, you must have a Godly motive and reason to go without food.

A Regular Fast or Normal Fast: Normally, a regular fast means refraining from eating all food. Most people still drink water during a regular fast. Fasting times are usually from 6.00am to 6.00pm but depending on your capability you can break your fast at your chosen time between 12.00 noon and 6.00pm. The duration could be for any number of days. Because the day starts at 12.00 midnight, normally, you would not have had any food after then.

A Full Fast or Dry Fast: This is a complete fast with abstention from food and drink. Following his encounter with Jesus on the road to Damascus, Paul went on a full fast for three days.

> *"And he was three days without sight, and neither did eat nor drink"*
>
> Acts 9:9

In the book of Esther, Queen Esther called for this type of fast:

> *"Then Esther bade them return Mordecai this answer, Go, gather together all the Jews that are present in Shushan, and fast ye for me, and neither eat nor drink three days, night or day: I also and my maidens will fast likewise; and so will I go in unto*

*the king, which is not according to the law: and if I
perish, I perish"*

Esther 4:15-16:

It is recommended that this type of fast be done with
extreme caution and not for extended periods of time.

A Partial Fast – This type of fast generally refers to
abstaining from food possibly for more than three days.
With this fast you can drink water and juice and eat fruits
or vegetables.

*"At that time I, Daniel, mourned for three weeks. I
ate no choice food; no meat or wine touched my lips;
and I used no lotions at all until the three weeks were
over"*

Daniel 10:2-3

Fasting is for a spiritual *purpose* without which you will be
dieting or just starving yourself. When breaking a fast, start
with something light (beverage or juice) before eating a
heavier meal. Failure to do so could lead to stomach complications such as cramps and indigestion.

A Sexual Fast:

> *"The husband should fulfil his marital duty to his wife, and likewise the wife to her husband. The wife's body does not belong to her alone but also to her husband. In the same way, the husband's body does not belong to him alone but also to his wife. Do not deprive each other except by mutual consent and for a time, so that you may devote yourselves to prayer. Then come together again so that Satan will not tempt you because of your lack of self-control."*
>
> 1 Corinthians 7:3-6

From the old testament to the New Testament fasting has always been a spiritual activity to sharpen your spirit man. Jesus fasted for forty days and He went on to tell us that there are some problems and issues that are irresolvable except by fasting and prayer. In 2 Samuel 12:16, David fasted when the child he had with Bathsheba was seriously ill. In Daniel 9:3, Daniel fasted for the enforcement of the prophetic decree by Prophet Jeremiah. In Jonah 3:5, the whole city of Nineveh fasted for God to forgive them of their sins upon hearing the preaching of Jonah. Fasting increases the sharpness of your spirit and makes your spirit strong. It is through fasting that different encounters happen.

I've been asked over and over again by many believers why

they have strange dreams when they embarked on a spiritual journey of fasting. It is a sign of victory as God reveals things to you that were hidden and that fasting has caused you to triumph. In Luke 4:1-13, Jesus, full of the Holy Spirit, returned from the Jordan and was led by the Spirit in the desert, where for forty days he was tempted by the devil.

In the Beatitudes, there is a story of a man who brought his sick child to the disciples of Jesus Christ for prayer. I will explain, now, the cases or issues where you should pray and fast.

"Lord, have mercy on my son: for he is lunatick, and sore vexed: for ofttimes he falleth into the fire, and oft into the water"

Matthew 17:15

"And one of the multitude answered and said, Master, I have brought unto thee my son, which hath a dumb spirit; And wheresoever he taketh him, he teareth him: and he foameth, and gnasheth with his teeth, and pineth away: and I spake to thy disciples that they should cast him out; and they could not"

Mark 9:17-18

"And, behold, a man of the company cried out, saying, Master, I beseech thee, look upon my son: for he is

> *mine only child. And, lo, a spirit taketh him, and he*
> *suddenly crieth out; and it teareth him that he*
> *foameth again, and bruising him hardly departeth*
> *from him"*
>
> Luke 9:38-39

The disciples attempted to cast out the evil spirit from the boy but they did not succeed and the boy did not get healed. Only after the father brought the boy before Jesus, who rebuked the evil spirit, was the boy healed. Later the disciples asked Jesus why they could not cast the evil spirit out of the boy.

> *"Howbeit this kind goeth not out but by prayer and*
> *fasting".*
>
> Matthew 17:21

Many people ask how they can tell that a particular situation needs both fasting and prayer. I will use the Scripture to explain. The Beatitudes have different accounts. We will take a go one at a time to show clearly which situations and issues may need both fasting and prayers.

In Matthew's account, the boy is a *lunatic*. The word lunatic in the Thesaurus is translated as meaning a state of being insane, disordered, unsound, abnormal, crazy, mad, incoherent, delusional, etc. Any situation that causes you to lose your peace calls for fasting. For example, situations such as disappointment in relationships, divorce, loss of something precious, betrayal, rejection, denial, etc.

The boy's situation also caused him to be sore vexed. Vexation is the state of being insensible and in pain. Any situation that causes you to be vexed and much troubled or to suffer unnecessarily, demands fasting. For example, when you are constantly in need of something or anxious about something, you are vexed and troubled.

We also read in Matthew, another affliction the boy experienced, that the evil spirit caused, was to be thrown in fire and water. Fire in this case can be described as being destructive, terrible and consuming. Water in the boy's situation can be described as oblivion, depression, and bitterness. My beloved reader, fire and water are two extreme objects and substances. Anytime you find yourself in an extreme situation and your troubles are over the limit you may need to fast and pray. For example, extreme cases of lack, unexplainable behaviour of a child, problems that cause shock like armed robbery, murder, serious medical conditions, etc.

In the Gospel of Mark, the evil spirit was described as *dumb*. The state of being dumb is to be without a voice, to be suppressed or smothered, to be put to silence, to be tongue tied, therefore not having the expression of speech. A situation that causes you to experience the above may require fasting. Problems such as recurrent court cases, imprisonment, and injustices such as slander, speculation, accusation, misrepresentation and character assassination may all call for fasting and prayer. When these things happen to you they cause you to feel embarrassment and shame and cause you to lose your self-esteem. Such injustices can be seen in marriages and relationships where one of the spouses is a cheat and should be dealt with spiritually.

In the Gospel of Mark, St. Mark wrote that the evil spirit *takes him*. In this case the word *"take"* means to apprehend, to capture, to seize, to possess, and to deprive. In a situation where you are seized, controlled, overpowered and unable to enjoy your God given liberty and freedom, may require fasting and prayer. These are situations where you are not yourself and your life is directed and driven and influenced by negative forces such as depression, anger, nightmares, harassment in the work place, etc.

St. Mark also wrote that the evil spirit *tears him*. To tear is to disjoint, to detach, to break, to dismember, to part, sever, to destroy. Situations where you or your efforts are not regarded may require fasting and prayer. These are problems that you encounter that cause people to treat you like rubbish or a door mat and they just walk all over you. You lose your integrity, respect and reputation. Undermining situations, where you used to command respect but you are no longer regarded and people who used to respect you don't even give you a chance to express yourself. This could be in situations such as in a marriage where the spouse has lost respect for the partner, in the work place, etc.

Another affliction the evil spirit caused the boy to experience was *foaming*. Foaming is associated with a violation of the body in the manner of agitation and violent shaking. Foaming at the mouth is also a sign of disgrace because saliva coming out of a person's mouth is disgusting to look at. Situation that causes you disgrace are disgusting situations, and therefore may require fasting and prayer. Also since saliva is supposed to be concealed rather been revealed, situations that cause a secret to be exposed and cause people to interfere with your business, situation that make you subject of public ridicule and criticism example such as criminal convictions, poverty, debt, etc all calls for Prayer and Fasting.

The evil spirit also caused the boy to experience *gnashing*. The word gnash is associated with resentment, displeasure, anger, wrath, indignation, vexation and bitterness. Gnashing of teeth is a sign of torment. Any situation that causes you torment may require fasting and prayer. You might be looking very good on the outside but hurting and in pain on the inside. For example, sickness and disease, grief, accidents, deformity, bitterness, depression, etc.

The evil spirit caused the boy to *pine*. In this case pining is associated with mental suffering, pain displeasure, dissatisfaction, discomfort, discomposure, vexation of spirit, discontentment and weariness. Situations that cause this kind of pining may require fasting and prayer. For example, such situations could be extreme delays, lack, infertility, marriage, etc.

St. Luke wrote that the evil spirit caused the boy to *cry out*. The word cry is associated with many different situations. One could cry out in pain, physical or emotional, there is also crying out in protest or frustration, and there is also crying out for mercy in a seemingly hopeless situation. Whatever situation causes you to shed tears or to weep, any problem that takes away your happiness and joy may require fasting and prayer. For example, the loss of loved ones or something important and dear in one's life, would call for prayer and fasting.

The account of St Luke also tells us that the evil spirit was *bruising* the boy. To bruise is to cause harm, hurt, to wound, to mutilate, to damage or to injure. Bruising can be caused to us both emotionally and physically. Any situation that affects you as described above may call for fasting and prayer. For example, all forms of physical and emotional abuse, vehicle accidents, verbal abuse, etc. Such situations can be found in marriages, in the work place, in a family where one sibling is mistreated, or even at school or in a community or environment where one is bullied or discriminated against.

The evil spirit was said to *hardly depart from him*. This

refers to situations with long-term effects; for example, chronic diseases or bad behaviour and stubbornness in a child. Addictive behaviour such as smoking, drinking and drug abuse also falls into this category.

The father of the afflicted boy is also affected because sons in those times were inheritors. This means they were to continue and carry on with the family business, customs and values. Any situation that is aimed at you and threatens your future may require fasting and prayer. Anything that causes your future to look uncertain or bleak requires spiritual insight. I am speaking about situations that will terminate your future such as premature death, cancerous and terminal sicknesses and disease, an attack on your dreams and vision, goals and aspirations.

Last but not least, the Bible tells us that the boy was the father's *only child*. This means there are some troubles that have been affecting you since you were young and you are still fighting them in your adulthood. Beloved reader, only you know the issues you have battled since you were young and just can't seem to stop no matter how hard you have tried.

The other strong word used to qualify the child is *"only"*. When you have only one child, they are something very precious to you. Circumstances can take away what is precious to you; steal your hope, joy and peace, possibly your future. For example, barrenness or situations that prevent a couple from getting the fruit of the womb, problems affecting your children.

The disciples tried and they could not cast the evil spirit out of the boy. However, when the boy was brought to Jesus, the Gospel of Mark says, the scribes were disputing the disciples. Any situation that causes controversy, chaos and misunderstanding is to be tackled by prayer and fasting.

My beloved, you now know that when Jesus Christ says this kind needs fasting and prayers what type and kinds of situations and circumstances he means. Most importantly you know that whatever you are going through, there is a solution to it and there is no situation that cannot be healed. All things are possible with God.

I have heard testimonies of how people used to die frequently and prematurely in my mother's family. At least every two years, two people in her family would die under strange circumstances. When I checked her family history, I discovered a long standing negative family altar in her family. I started having revelations concerning my mother, revealing the Enemy's plots to attack her life. I embarked on a thirty day fast to stop this situation, not only to protect my mother but for total deliverance from premature death for the whole family. I now can say to the Glory of God that her family is now free from premature death, in Jesus name.

Chapter 4

Prophetic Instructions (Prophetic Signs and Tokens)

When a prophetic word is released, in order for the full manifestation of the word, there are different forms of instructions that can be followed in order to show obedience, conviction and respect for the word. These instructions and directives help in the activation of the prophecy. In order for the transition from "it shall come to pass" to "it has come to pass" one must follow the prophetic direction given precisely. There are many instructions that are associated with the prophetic including, signs, tokens, offerings and sacrifices found in the Holy Bible. In both the Old Testament and the New Testament, especially in the Ministry of Christ, signs and tokens were used to fulfil the purposes of God. Signs and tokens do not make sense naturally but obedience and labour can bring about the manifestation of miracles and testimonies. Signs and tokens are symbolic objects and substances that are used to activate a prophetic word and to seal a miracle with its foundation from the Holy Bible backed by the power of the most High GOD.

In Exodus chapter 4, God first asked Moses what he had in his hand. Moses had a staff which he used to care for his herd and for stability as he walked. God asked Moses to throw it down, to let go of it regardless of Moses' need of it. God wants what is in your hands, no matter how important it is to you.

In verse 3, Moses throws down the staff and when it touches the ground it turns into a snake, and he runs from it. At this point he didn't have his staff to protect himself from the snake. But then God tells him to pick it up by the tail! Logic tells us that picking up the snake by the tail leaves it with ample flexibility to curl up and twist and bite. It makes more sense to pin the snake to the ground by the back of its neck and pick it up from there. However, Moses obeyed and reached out and took hold of the snake by the tail and it turned back into a staff in his hand.

In verse 6, God gives Moses a second sign by telling him to put his hand inside his cloak. Moses did so and when he took it out, it was leprous, like snow. Leprous diseases were contagious and defiling, a person with leprosy was isolated, a social and even family outcast. God then told Moses to put his hand back into his cloak and when he took it out, it was restored, and like the rest of his flesh.

"That they may believe that the LORD God of their

fathers, the God of Abraham, the God of Isaac, and the God of Jacob, hath appeared unto thee. ⁸And it shall come to pass, if they will not believe thee, neither hearken to the voice of the first sign, that they will believe the voice of the latter sign. ⁹And it shall come to pass, if they will not believe also these two signs, neither hearken unto thy voice, that thou shalt take of the water of the river, and pour it upon the dry land: and the water which thou takest out of the river shall become blood upon the dry land"

Exodus 4:5, 8-9

Further on, in Exodus chapter 4, we read about Moses performing the signs that God asked him to, in order to bring about first belief to His people. It is important that we, God's people first believe.

²⁹And Moses and Aaron went and gathered together all the elders of the children of Israel:
³⁰And Aaron spake all the words which the LORD had spoken unto Moses, and did the signs in the sight of the people. ³¹And the people believed: and when they heard that the LORD had visited the children of Israel, and that he had looked upon their affliction, then they bowed their heads and worshipped.

Exodus 4:29-31

In Exodus chapter 7, the first sign God gave to Moses is performed by Aaron and Moses in the presence of the Egyptians.

> *⁸And the LORD spake unto Moses and unto Aaron, saying,*
> *⁹When Pharaoh shall speak unto you, saying, Shew a miracle for you: then thou shalt say unto Aaron, Take thy rod, and cast it before Pharaoh, and it shall become a serpent. ¹⁰And Moses and Aaron went in unto Pharaoh, and they did so as the LORD had commanded: and Aaron cast down his rod before Pharaoh, and before his servants, and it became a serpent. ¹¹Then Pharaoh also called the wise men and the sorcerers: now the magicians of Egypt, they also did in like manner with their enchantments. ¹²For they cast down every man his rod, and they became serpents: but Aaron's rod swallowed up their rods.*
>
> Exodus 7:8-12

Although Moses had performed the first and second signs to the Israelites, as we read in Exodus 4:29-30, he had to wait until he got to Egypt to perform the third sign. Many more signs followed the deliverance of the children of Israel from Egypt but the crossing of the red sea was the one that totally released them from Egyptian captivity.

²¹And Moses stretched out his hand over the sea; and the LORD caused the sea to go back by a strong east wind all that night, and made the sea dry land, and the waters were divided. ²²And the children of Israel went into the midst of the sea upon the dry ground: and the waters were a wall unto them on their right hand, and on their left. ²³And the Egyptians pursued, and went in after them to the midst of the sea, even all Pharaoh's horses, his chariots, and his horsemen. ²⁴And it came to pass, that in the morning watch the LORD looked unto the host of the Egyptians through the pillar of fire and of the cloud, and troubled the host of the Egyptians, ²⁵And took off their chariot wheels, that they drave them heavily: so that the Egyptians said, Let us flee from the face of Israel; for the LORD fighteth for them against the Egyptians. ²⁶And the LORD said unto Moses, Stretch out thine hand over the sea, that the waters may come again upon the Egyptians, upon their chariots, and upon their horsemen. ²⁷And Moses stretched forth his hand over the sea, and the sea returned to his strength when the morning appeared; and the Egyptians fled against it; and the LORD overthrew the Egyptians in the midst of the sea. ²⁸And the waters returned, and covered the chariots, and the horsemen, and all the host of Pharaoh that came into

the sea after them; there remained not so much as one of them. ²⁹But the children of Israel walked upon dry land in the midst of the sea; and the waters were a wall unto them on their right hand, and on their left. ³⁰Thus the LORD saved Israel that day out of the hand of the Egyptians; and Israel saw the Egyptians dead upon the sea shore. ³¹And Israel saw that great work which the LORD did upon the Egyptians: and the people feared the LORD, and believed the LORD, and his servant Moses.

Exodus 14:21-31

It is not possible for a common staff to divide the Red Sea into half but by the power of God, all things are possible. When operating using signs and tokens, it's the belief and faith behind it that causes the miracles to happen. Let me give an awesome testimony associated of the signs and tokens God wrought through me.

In 2006, I met a woman who had one son and after nine years, although she desired to have more children, she couldn't because she had stopped menstruating. She and her husband had sought medical treatment and they were told that the husband had a low sperm count, and given his condition it would be very difficult for her to conceive. When she told me her story, we prayed and God gave me a prophetic instruction for the couple to follow. I asked her to bring me two oranges and after we prayed, I asked her to eat one of the oranges and to take the second one to her husband to eat. From the perspective of common sense, this would seem foolish. I later told her that the oranges I had asked them to eat were a sign of heavenly strength being pushed into their systems to help them be fruitful and productive and that God would give them two sons.

Although they were believers, it sounded so strange to them but without any hesitation they obeyed. After five months, the woman called me and told me that she was pregnant. She later gave birth to a bouncing baby boy and by the grace of God, two years later she had another son. It's not the orange that did something but their belief and faith in what they had done that brought the miracle.

Prophet Elisha in 2 Kings 2:19-20, asked the inhabitants of Jericho to bring to him salt in a bowl and he prayed using the salt to heal the waters that were causing miscarriages. Salt was a common commodity but why didn't they do it before the prophet came? Specific instructions are only given by the power of the Holy Spirit to the prophets of God. In 2 Kings 5, Naaman, a commander of an army, suffered from leprosy. When Naaman went to Prophet Elisha, Elisha asked Naaman to go and wash in the Jordan River seven times. When Naaman obeyed, he was immediately healed.

Before Naaman washing in the Jordan River, he was upset about the instruction given to him because the Jordan River was muddy, and thus dirtier than the clear and clean waters in his hometown of Damascus. Sometimes the prophetic instructions might seem foolish and make no sense but it is God using the least likely means to bring about our much-anticipated miracle. In 2 Kings 6, when the sons of the prophets were cutting wood to build their shelters, we read that the iron axe-head that they used fell into the River Jordan. When the man cried out to Prophet Elisha, for the tool was borrowed, he didn't pray but threw a stick where the axe-had had sunk and made the iron float. It was a miracle because metal cannot float as it has to obey the laws of nature but by the use of a token, Prophet Elisha was able to beat the natural laws using the supernatural.

Furthermore, in Ezekiel 37, Prophet Ezekiel prophesied the dry bones were a symbol and signs to denote the army of the nation of Israel. In John 9:6 in the New Testament, Jesus healed a blind man by mixing sand with his saliva. From the perspective of common sense, such an act would be looked upon with disgust but because it carried a prophetic mystery, the blind man received his sight. The reason for sand and spittle is simple, God created man from the dust of the Earth. Since the spittle is something that is disgusting, Jesus was taking the blind man back to his creation and into the original intent of God for his life. Since man was created in the image of God, and in the image of God there is no blindness, the man's blindness was cured.

The saliva depicts the disgusting condition of blindness affecting the man. Jesus had the power to take him back into the original plan of God for his life. In Mark 7:33 Jesus healed a deaf man by touching the man's ears and tongue with his finger that had saliva upon it.

In John 8, Jesus upon delivering the woman who was caught in the act of adultery from the hands of her accusers, stooped down and with his finger wrote on the ground. He lets us understand that no matter what the condition or how far you've travelled in your mess, Jesus can still reach you and take you out of it. In Acts 19:12, in the ministry of the Apostles, we read that God did extraordinary miracles through Paul, so that even handkerchiefs and aprons that had touched him were taken to the sick, and their illnesses were cured and the evil spirits left them. In Acts 5:15, we read that people brought the sick into the streets and laid them on beds and mats so that at least Peter's shadow might fall on some of them as he passed by. The shadow of peter would fall on people and they would be healed. God works in many ways and uses signs, symbols, tokens, etc. to perform His works. In Mark 6:41, Jesus took five loaves of bread and two fishes, He blessed and broke the loaves and gave them to his disciples to set before the multitude who all ate and were filled. The five loaves of bread and two fishes were symbols of the great abundance and supply that God provided from Heaven. Never despise prophetic instructions because it is your obedience that determines whether you believe or doubt the prophetic word.

Offerings and Sacrifices

The last aspect of the prophetic instructions involves offerings and sacrifices. I want to urge you, my dear reader, to never meet a man of God or a prophet empty handed. Your offering or sacrifice provokes the anointing of the servant of God to release heavenly blessings over your life. When a prophetic word is released, God can either direct the prophet on a specific offering or sacrifice that needs to be released based on the particular word. The Prophet of God will give you specific direction. As an example, he could direct you to give to give an offering to your church, to the Prophet or sometimes by giving an offering to charity.

In 1 Samuel 9, we read about the conversation Saul had with his servant before they made their way to the man of God.

> *⁷Then said Saul to his servant, But, behold, if we go, what shall we bring the man? for the bread is spent in our vessels, and there is not a present to bring to the man of God: what have we? ⁸And the servant answered Saul again, and said, Behold, I have here at hand the fourth part of a shekel of silver: that will I give to the man of God, to tell us our way."*
>
> 1 Samuel 9:7-8

They knew the power of prophecy and how important it is to honour the servants of God. Before the word is released, the servant of God needs to be honoured for the office in which he stands but also to tap into God's blessings. Nowadays, many people have problems with seed offering and sacrifice, both believers and non-believers, because not enough time is given to its explanation for us to really understand its benefits. Until servants of God take time to teach this principle to people, it will always be seen as a platform to raise issues in the Body of Christ. There are some preachers who use this as an opportunity to outwit vulnerable people who are desperate for a miracle and thus take advantage of them. I believe that when the right channel is used there will be no objections raised. Some prophets have taken it in the wrong way and some take it by manipulative means with no explanations or biblical foundations.

I believe that when people are taught the significance of offerings and the power behind offerings, it will naturally become the habit and character of people to give. In 2 Kings 5, Naaman, who had a misconception about the operations of the prophets and the worship of God, before he came to the prophet Elisha, he had prepared serious offerings to give to the man of God. Before he received his healing, Naaman knew the significance of an offering and by faith he had already prepared it before he made his journey to the man of God. This teaches us a great lesson that by faith we should give, not only after we have been delivered from our problems but even before.

"¹⁵And he returned to the man of God, he and all his company, and came, and stood before him: and he said, Behold, now I know that there is no God in all the earth, but in Israel: now therefore, I pray thee, take a blessing of thy servant. ¹⁶But he said, As the LORD liveth, before whom I stand, I will receive none. And he urged him to take it; but he refused. ¹⁷And Naaman said, Shall there not then, I pray thee, be given to thy servant two mules' burden of earth? for thy servant will henceforth offer neither burnt offering nor sacrifice unto other gods, but unto the LORD"

2 Kings 5:15-17

In 2 Samuel 24:24, when David sinned and there was a serious calamity in the land of Israel, what saved him was the sacrificial offering he gave. When the angel of death responsible for destroying the people got to the threshing floor where the sacrifice was made, the angel stopped and that brought peace back to the land. Sacrifices are important in stopping calamities. I want to urge you, my beloved reader, that if there has been any long term calamity and crisis you have been encountering, start making your journey to sacrifice to God and I can guarantee you that there will be a miracle in your life. A sacrificial offering is something that means something to us, something important to us. When people willingly and perceptively participate in sacrificial offerings, they acknowledge the important principle of God's authority over their lives, determined by the procedure He prescribed.

In Genesis 22:2, God asked Abraham to sacrifice Isaac not Ishmael. Isaac was Abraham's source of joy, happiness, hope and encouragement but God demanded him for a sacrifice. The meaning of Isaac in the Hebrew is laughter, so God was asking Abraham to offer his source of laughter. Anytime God asks you for a sacrifice, He is only demanding your source of laughter through something that makes you happy. For example, your possessions, your treasure, your finances, etc. to know whether you love him more than these things.

"Gather my saints together unto me; those that have made a covenant with me by sacrifice"
Psalm 50:5

Sacrifice is the foundation of every covenant, as seen in the above scripture. The covenant we have with God is what makes us His true children. Obedience in offering and sacrifice is what causes the abundance of God to be fulfilled in our lives and to never cease, as it is written in Luke 6:38, "Give and it shall be given unto you." There was a woman whom I prayed for and her concern was for God to deliver hers and her family from the spirit of death. She told me that anytime she went to sleep, she would dream that she was at a funeral. At the time she talked to me about these dreams, her husband was seriously ill and doctors had given him only a few days to live. When I prayed with her, I learned from the realm of the spirit, by the prophetic anointing over my life, the root cause of what was happening to her family was coming from a particular town. I called her and the name of the town. She confirmed that it was her hometown in Nigeria and God revealed to me the name of the person who was behind it, who was being used as an agent of the devil. The lady knew the person.

I gave her a prophetic direction to sow a sacrificial offering and we embarked on prayer and fasting to destroy the root cause and to reverse the attacks on the woman. Psalm 34:21 says, evil shall slay the wicked man and he that hates the righteous shall be desolate. It was later revealed in a vision, while we were praying, that the person responsible for the wickedness against the woman and her family, who was being manipulated by evil spirits, would suffer the very shame and death that was designed against this family. The woman told me that the sacrificial offering she gave was the greatest offerings she had ever given.

Three days into our spiritual journey of prayer and fasting, she told me that the dreams of funerals had ceased.